To my daughters,
always use your power to evoke change!

Mrs. Jessica says, "Good morning class!"

"Good morning Mrs. Jessica!" The class responds in unison.

"Do you know what today is?!" She says with excitement.

"It is field trip day. My mom said that
we are going to the movie theatre."

"That's right! Everyone brought their $5 for special snacks too. When we go to the theatre each one of you will talk to the employee behind the register and order your food. Just like how you do when we go to the restaurant. Before we leave, everyone line up to go potty and I'll pack extra batteries and extra clothes."

"Ready? I have got the permission slips, extra batteries, the FM system, and clothes. Let's rock and roll!"

Everyone piles out of the classroom rushing
down the ramp to the school buses.

We get strapped into our harnesses
and off to the movies we go.

We sing songs on the bus and can hear Mrs. Jessica
pretty well since she's wearing the FM System.

Some of my friends nod off for a few.
I must admit, the lull of the bus makes me sleepy too.

We have arrived. The bus driver unlatches us
from the seatbelt harness and we
spill out of the bus in sheer excitement.

Mrs. Jessica is trying to corral us and is fussing at Mario
as he wonders off. We ALL hear her in the FM System.

We get to the ticket window and hand the attendant our money and get a ticket for the movie in return.

We then go to the concession counter to order our snacks.

"It's too loud in here, I can't understand what she's saying."

"Then what is something we can do to
help you hear better?" Mrs. Jessica asks.

"Can I give her the FM microphone so I can hear her better?"

"Of course! What a great solution."

Zeina is still struggling to hear the attendant clearly, but she doesn't want it to seem obvious, so she tries to read her lips and just says, "I want what they're having."

We get our snacks and head toward the theatre when suddenly,
Zeina realizes she is missing her cochlear implant.

"Um, Mrs. Jessica? I can't find my cochlear implant."
Zeina breaks down and is crying hysterically.

She's worried her parents will be mad,
she's worried Mrs. Jessica will be mad,
and mostly, she's worried she won't be
able to hear the movie like everyone else.

As a super HEARo team, we are ready to take action.
We will use our gifts to aid in the situation
and come up with a solution.

To figure out where Zeina may have lost it,
we need her to calm down so we can talk.
I give my friend a hug and start deep breathing with her.

Mario takes Elise and they zip and zoom to retrace all our steps.

They go to the ticket counter and all they
find is old gum stuck to the bottom of the counter.

Ally checks the bathroom, and almost slips in
the puddle of water on the floor. She didn't see it.

They are scouring high and low to no avail.

Malcolm is rocking back and forth because
Zeina is crying loudly and he does not
like loud noises, they overwhelm him.

Mrs. Jessica is trying to calm Malcolm
by offering his noise cancelling headphones.

Then suddenly, I remember what we learned in class!
We can use the close caption reader.

Mrs. Jessica has been teaching us how to
read and how to use closed captioning.

"Mrs. Jessica, Mrs. Jessica!! I've got it!
Let's ask the for the closed captioning readers!"

Mrs. Jessica: "Great Idea! Let me go get you all
settled in the theatre, I'll set up the readers
and I'll keep looking for Zeina's implant."

Zeina calms down some as we head to our seats.
We are all set up and the movie begins.
Thankfully we didn't miss much when looking for Zeina's CI.

The closed captioning readers worked great.
We can't read all the words yet, but it helps fill in some of
what we miss and she still has her hearing aid in her other ear.

Mrs. Jessica comes back to the theatre and no luck. She didn't find Zeina's CI.

We try to enjoy the rest of the movie, but we are ALL a little anxious.
Our equipment is expensive and sometimes hard to keep up with.

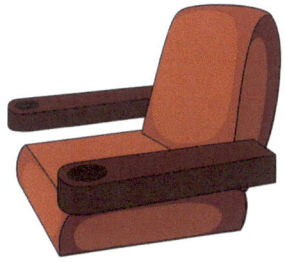

After the movie, we quietly walked back to the bus.
We get back in our harnesses and rest our heads on the side of the bus.
We hear the click-clack of the bus as we ride back to school.

CLICK CLACK  CLICK CLACK

Malcom asks, "what is THAT noise?"

He looks and sure enough, the click-clack was
Zeina's cochlear implant bouncing on the bus.

The magnet must have gotten stuck on the bus when
she leaned her head against it on the way to the theatre.

Everyone on the bus cheered in excitement!
The one thing that is so great about our special
class is that we all bond over our exceptionalities.

When Zeina lost her cochlear implant, it was like all of us had too.
We have all been in Zeina's shoes before when it comes to missing equipment.

Thankfully, we always have each other's backs,
like true Super HEARos do!

# Vocabulary Page:

**BAHA (Bone Anchored Hearing Aid) or a bone conduction hearing aid-** an alternative to a traditional behind-the-ear hearing aid for people with Microtia and/or Atresia. BAHAs are surgically implanted or worn on a soft band strap, similar to Billie. The hearing aid is made to pick up sound and pass it using bone conduction to the inner ear.

**Microtia-** Latin for "little ear". The outer ear doesn't fully form in utero. There are four types of Microtia, ranging from Type 1 to Type 4. Type 1 is the mildest form, where the ear retains its normal shape, but is smaller than usual. Type 4 is the most severe type where the entire pinna is missing.

**Deaf-** Hearing loss so severe that there is little to no residual hearing, usually due to inner ear or nerve damage. It may be caused by a congenital defect, injury, disease, certain medications, excessive exposure to loud noise, or due to age. A cochlear implant can be an option for auditory access to process speech sounds for some.

**Hard of Hearing-** Hearing loss that is less. There may be enough residual hearing that an auditory device, such as a hearing aid, provides assistance and access to process speech.

**Hijab-** A veil covering hair from men, besides immediate family, in the Muslim faith/culture. It is a symbol of modesty.

**Cochlear Implant-** A cochlear implant is used to amplify and clarify sounds and allow auditory access. There is an internal and external component. The internal component is surgically implanted into the cochlea to stimulate the auditory nerve. The external component is responsible for picking up sounds to send to the internal component.

**Hearing Aid-** An electronic device worn behind the ear used to amplify sound.

## Vocabulary Page:

**FM System-** A wireless device that assists a person utilizing a hearing device or who is hard of hearing, by overcoming the obstacle of distance from the speaker or noisy environments.

**Afro-** The word is derived from Afro-American. It is the natural growth of curly textured hair, in any length kinky hair texture.

**ADA-** Americans with Disabilities Act. Per the ADA guidelines: The Final Rule requires require movie theaters to: have and maintain the equipment necessary to provide closed movie captioning and audio description at a movie patron's seat whenever showing a digital movie produced, distributed, or otherwise made available with these features; provide notice to the public about the availability of these features; and ensure that theater staff is available to assist patrons with the equipment before, during, and after the showing of a movie with these features.